The**Cornell**Lab of Ornithology

America's Favorite Birds

40 Beautiful Birds to Color

Miyoko Chu
Brenda Lyons

The**Cornell**Lab
Publishing Group

Text by Miyoko Chu
Design by Patricia N Gonzalez

ISBN: 978-1-943645-41-1

Printed in China

Library of Congress Cataloging-in-Publication Data available.

10 9 8 7 6 5 4 3 2 1

Produced by the
Cornell Lab Publishing Group
120A North Salem Street
Apex, NC 27502

www.CornellLabpg.com

By buying products with the FSC label you
are supporting the growth of responsible
forest management worldwide.

MIX
Paper from
responsible sources
FSC® C124385

Introduction

North America has more than 700 bird species, each one beautiful and fascinating in its own right, each one a living work of art. Choosing 40 favorites was a daunting prospect, but we knew whom we could count on for help.

To choose the birds in this book, we listened to the Cornell Lab of Ornithology's community of more than one million bird enthusiasts. For the first 15 species, we looked to the winners of our annual March Migration Madness competitions (2011–15). We guaranteed a page for every bird that made it from the "Tweet 16" to the "Feathered Four" in head-to-head voting by the Cornell Lab's Facebook fans. In 2016, our Facebook fans and eNewsletter subscribers cast more than 250,000 votes to select an additional 15 species.

Rounding out the selection, the Cornell Lab picked the remaining 10 species to include diverse birds from across North America's spectacular landscapes—birds we felt people would love to see in a coloring book, even if a few of these species didn't quite win the popular votes.

What do these favorite birds have in common? Some are wildly colorful, such as the Painted Bunting, splashed with green, blue, and red—or the Wood Duck, its plumage a masterpiece of bold color and design. Others, such as the Tufted Titmouse and White-breasted Nuthatch, may be modest in appearance, but they win hearts and votes because they enliven our backyards and neighborhoods throughout the seasons. The world just wouldn't be the same without them.

Yet some of the favorite birds in this book nearly did disappear from many North American landscapes in the past century, including the

This book is dedicated to everyone who sees beauty in birds.

Bald Eagle, Peregrine Falcon, and Atlantic Puffin. With support from the public, and tremendous efforts from scientists, conservationists, and lawmakers, these birds have made a heartening comeback in recent decades. With greater protection from commercial hunting and habitat loss, many other species have rebounded, too, including Wood Ducks, Great Blue Herons, and Sandhill Cranes.

Their stories give hope for so many other bird species whose numbers are still declining—birds such as the Red Knot and other shorebirds that travel the globe; colorful songsters such as the Painted Bunting; and specialized birds of the open West, including the iconic Greater Sage-Grouse. By celebrating these birds, we reaffirm together that they are worth saving. They are some of nature's most breathtaking expressions of beauty and vivid examples of the interconnectedness among people, wildlife, and nature.

As you bring color and imagination to these pages, we hope you discover something new about your own favorite birds in this book— or find inspiration to add a few more favorites to your list. We hope you'll enjoy hours of relaxation exploring the birds and habitats featured here, and that you'll go back outside often to look for birds there, too, living the moments that become new memories to treasure and share.

—Miyoko Chu and Brenda Lyons

Acknowledgments

We thank the Cornell Lab of Ornithology's community of bird enthusiasts from around the world for casting your votes to select the birds for this book. All of the photographs in this book were donated by members of the Cornell Lab of Ornithology's Birdshare Flickr group. We thank the photographers for their generosity as acknowledged in the credits along with their photos on the back page. Special thanks to Dr. Kevin McGowan who shared his insights on concepts and illustrations. He helped us tremendously, and any remaining flaws are our own. Charles Dardia and the Cornell University Museum of Vertebrates graciously granted access for Brenda Lyons to examine birds in the collection. Brenda also thanks the Horizon Wings raptor rehabilitation center, which has helped her learn about birds through the years. We thank our many collaborators for their support and insights, including Mary Guthrie, Diane Tessaglia-Hymes, Mya Thompson, Victoria Campbell, Andrew Leach, Hans Teensma, and designer Patricia Gonzalez. Our heartfelt thanks to Brian Sockin, whose boundless vision, creativity, and enthusiasm have made this book possible. Finally, we thank our families and friends for their support: David Lyons, Jennifer Campbell-Smith, Mark and Tilden Chao, and Francesca, Berbie, and David Chu.

Learn more about birds

with the Cornell Lab of Ornithology

The Cornell Lab of Ornithology is a nonprofit organization dedicated to improving the understanding and protection of birds. **Our hallmarks are scientific excellence and technological innovation to advance the understanding of nature and to engage people of all ages in learning about birds and protecting the planet.**

Beyond the pages of this book, we hope you'll enjoy these 10 ways to keep learning more about birds.

1. Identify birds with the Merlin Bird ID app.
It's exciting to see a new bird, especially when you can clinch the identification! For help, download the free Merlin Bird ID app. Merlin will ask you five questions to help you identify the birds around you. Merlin.AllAboutBirds.org

2. Delve into a wealth of information using All About Birds.
Learn more about your favorite birds on the All About Birds website. Explore fascinating facts, sounds, photos, range maps, and more. AllAboutBirds.org

3. Take your understanding to the next level with the Cornell Lab Bird Academy.
Try fun online activities that teach you about bird biology, including behavior and anatomy. You can also sign up for courses ranging from bird identification webinars to the college-level Home Study Course in Bird Biology. Academy.AllAboutBirds.org

4. Enjoy live, close-up views with Bird Cams.
Watch as hawks, owls, and other birds raise their young. See colorful birds at locations across the country, featured on our feeder cams. Cams.AllAboutBirds.org

5. Watch birds and share what you see with a citizen-science project.
By recording your observations, you can contribute to science and conservation. The Cornell Lab invites you to participate in the Great Backyard Bird Count, Project FeederWatch, eBird, NestWatch, Celebrate Urban Birds, and YardMap. Birds.Cornell.edu

6. Explore the world's birds with the Macaulay Library.
Hear the sounds of wildlife from around the world or watch their behaviors in videos. Search for a bird you have in mind or browse hundreds of thousands of recordings. MacaulayLibrary.org

7. Share BirdSleuth with a child or a teacher.
The BirdSleuth K–12 curriculum engages kids in scientific inquiry and learning about birds outdoors. You can get your school interested in birds or enjoy the activities with kids at home. BirdSleuth.org

8. Join the Cornell Lab's Facebook community.
Connect with others who love birds, and get your daily dose of bird quizzes, photos, and fun facts about birds. Facebook.com/Cornellbirds

9. Learn more about the fascinating lives of birds in *Living Bird* magazine.
Enjoy spectacular photographs of birds and gain new insights from in-depth articles. This quarterly magazine comes right to your mailbox when you join as a member of the Cornell Lab. Your support gives back to the birds by advancing the Lab's conservation mission. Birds.Cornell.edu/Join

10. Discover more about birds every month with Cornell Lab eNews.
It's easy to keep in touch with the latest news and ideas about birds. This free newsletter brings the beauty of birds right to your email box. Birds.Cornell.edu/eNews

American Goldfinches

and purple coneflowers

In summer, look for flocks of American Goldfinches alighting on coneflowers, asters, and thistle. Rather than feeding their young insects as most songbirds do, goldfinches partially digest seeds into a sticky semi-solid formula for their nestlings.

Goldfinches especially love thistle—they eat the seeds and use the fluff, or pappus, to line their nests. American Goldfinches often nest in July, later than other songbirds, perhaps because of their dependence on late-blooming thistle.

Pileated Woodpeckers

at their nest in a sugar maple

Young Pileated Woodpeckers grow up in a tree hole excavated by their parents. Pileated Woodpeckers use their chisel-like bills to chip away at the wood for several weeks to create the cavity where the female lays her eggs. She and her mate bring food to the cavity until the young fledge about 24–31 days after hatching.

The abandoned nest cavity becomes a valuable home for other animals, especially species such as ducks and owls that can't excavate their own. Boreal Owls, Northern Saw-whet Owls, Wood Ducks, Buffleheads, Barrow's Goldeneyes, squirrels, and bats are among at least 38 vertebrate species that use Pileated Woodpecker cavities.

Ruby-throated Hummingbirds

and trumpet vine flowers

Ruby-throated Hummingbirds love the flowers of trumpet vines, perhaps because these showy blooms offer more nectar than most other flowers. Each bloom produces nectar for just 20–30 hours. As the hummingbirds zip from flower to flower, they carry yellow pollen on their heads.

Hummingbirds are the trumpet vine's best pollinator. They transfer 10 times more pollen per visit than bumblebees do. Where hummingbirds visit more often, trumpet vines bear more fruit. Thus, the birds and blooms perpetuate one another—the flowers give sustenance, and the hummers help generate the next crop of flowers.

Wood Ducks

on hatching day

Wood Ducks are at home whether on the water, in trees, or flying through the sky. You might see the male with his dazzling plumage at a pond, or catch a glimpse of him and his mate high in a tree as they look for a cavity where she'll lay her eggs.

About 24 hours after the eggs hatch, the ducklings leap out into the world from their nest, which may be as high as 50 feet. If they don't make an aquatic landing, they bounce off the ground, then toddle after their mom to water.

Cedar Waxwings

eating serviceberries

When courting one another, Cedar Waxwings exchange the gift of a berry. The male hops sideways toward the female and presents her with the gift. She takes it, hops sideways, then hops back, and returns it to him. They may pass it back and forth a dozen times, hopping in between, until the female eats the berry.

Cedar Waxwings are unusual among songbirds because they eat mostly fruit. In winter, you might see flocks of waxwings descending on shrubs, and hear them calling with thin, high-pitched notes as they search for berries.

Snowy Owls

on the arctic tundra

Snowy Owls raise their young on the arctic tundra in summer. Soon after they learn to fly, the parents and their young travel their separate ways as solitary nomads across the arctic.

Scientists tracked two siblings from a nest in the Arctic Circle on Victoria Island, Canada. More than a year later, they discovered one of the young Snowy Owls in Clyde Forks, Canada, 2,100 miles southeast of the nest. They found its sibling in Sakhalin, Russia, 3,300 miles southwest of the nest.

Atlantic Puffins

on an offshore island

The Atlantic Puffin is a bird of the sea, returning to offshore islands only during the nesting season. Its bill, spectacular in shape and color, is an essential tool on water and on land. When a puffin chases after fish, it can clamp down on prey one at time until its bill holds a dozen fish or more. On land, the puffin nests in a rock crevice or digs its own burrow. Biting and scraping into the soil with its powerful bill, the puffin can excavate a tunnel 3–6 feet long with a chamber at the end for a single egg.

A puffin's bill changes colors with the seasons. It's brightest during spring and summer when it's time to court a mate and raise young. After breeding, colorful sheaths on the bill drop off, leaving the puffin with a plainer bill as it goes back to sea, where it will spend the next eight months.

Killdeer

with eggs

A Killdeer lays her eggs on the ground, camouflaged among stones, twigs, or grass. During courtship, she takes turns with her mate in creating a shallow depression with feet scraping and with body pressed against the ground.

After the eggs are laid, Killdeer may add light-colored objects such as pebbles, shells, or bones to the nest. When leaving the nest, they also toss material over their shoulder into the nest. Scientists counted 1,552 pebbles in one nest.

Western Tanager

and whitebark pine

Ornithologist Samuel Rathbun wrote that the song of a Western Tanager was "very pleasing, carrying a suggestion of the wildness and freedom of the woodland: not of the country that has felt the influence of mankind."

With its flaming red and yellow plumage, contrasted with the black of its wings and back, the Western Tanager is also one of the most dazzling songsters of western forests. Unlike its eastern cousin, the Scarlet Tanager, which converts yellow pigments from its diet into red pigments, the Western Tanager has a rare red pigment called rhodoxanthin, perhaps gained from eating insects that ingested the pigment from plants.

Barred Owl

in quaking aspen

Barred Owls live in mature and old-growth forests that offer diverse prey and large trees for nesting. The shade of old trees prevents new trees from growing, creating a more open understory where the owls can hunt for mammals, invertebrates, amphibians, birds, and fish. The forest canopy provides protection from extremes of weather, and extra cover to hide from other birds, which often mob the owls upon discovery.

The owls nest in tree cavities or in open nests abandoned by hawks, crows, or squirrels. These limited nesting sites are believed to influence the sedentary ways of Barred Owls. Of 158 owls banded by scientists, none was found to move farther than 7 miles.

Bald Eagle

over an Alaskan river

The majestic Bald Eagle is the national symbol of the United States. It can be found in every U.S. state except Hawaii, as well as across Canada, nesting in forested areas near water where it can hunt for fish and other prey. Bald Eagles may use the same territory for nesting year after year, and can live in the wild for more than 30 years.

Bald Eagles were in danger of extinction in 1963, with only 417 pairs left in the lower 48 states. Protections such as the Endangered Species Act and the banning of the pesticide DDT helped reverse declines from shooting, trapping, and poisoning. Thanks to the efforts of conservationists, lawmakers, and the public, Bald Eagles are making an extraordinary comeback.

Great Blue Heron

with cattails

A Great Blue Heron at a pond is the picture of grace and calm. Slowly and deliberately, it wades in search of fish and frogs, then strikes quickly with its bill.

The largest of North America's heron species, it stands 3–4 feet tall. As a young Great Blue Heron approaches adulthood, it grows long, showy feathers called "nuptial plumes" that extend from its crown and that hang from its breast and shoulders.

Blue Jay

and pin oak tree

A Blue Jay's bold blue color is not created by pigments but by the structure of its feathers. The pigment in the feathers is brown, but the cells on the surface of the feather barbs scatter light into blue.

In autumn, Blue Jays harvest acorns, beechnuts, and hickory nuts. They eat some but hide as many as 5,000 in a single autumn, burying them in the ground and often covering them with a pebble or leaf. Blue Jays have excellent memories for retrieving the nuts later, but even so, some nuts sprout, helping to regenerate forests.

Northern Cardinals

and winterberries

Bold in appearance but shy in personality, Northern Cardinals bring a splash of color year-round to woodlands and neighborhoods. To get their crimson feathers, cardinals must eat pigments found in berries, insects, and seeds. Brighter males defend territories that are dense with more plants, and they succeed in raising more young.

Females prefer to mate with bright males but their own plumage is in softer shades, more suited for camouflage when sitting on a nest.

Red-tailed Hawk

in flight

Red-tailed Hawks are one of North America's most commonly encountered birds of prey. They are widespread across open or partially wooded habitats, nesting on high structures from trees and cliffs to city buildings. In some areas, the male and female remain on their territory throughout the seasons and raise their young together year after year.

In spring, Red-tailed Hawks perform spectacular aerial courtship displays. The male and female grasp one another with their talons and spiral toward the ground before pulling apart.

Green Heron

hunting for fish

A log over water is a favorite perch for a Green Heron as it watches for fish. To help its chances, it sometimes uses a lure—a bread crust, mayfly, or feather. It holds the lure in its bill while watching, throws the bait in the water, then strikes when a fish comes near.

The Green-backed Heron, a close relative of the Green Heron, was once considered the same species. It has been observed breaking twigs to fashion into lures, making it one of only a few birds in the world that are known to use tools.

Northern Flicker

in a boxelder

With their bold and colorful plumage, Northern Flickers are an arresting sight in woodlands and backyards. Unlike other woodpeckers, which hammer holes in trees to look for insects, Northern Flickers pound into the ground to search for ants and beetles.

A flicker sometimes uses its bill to dig into anthills, extending its barbed tongue more than an inch beyond its bill to capture the ants and their larvae.

Belted Kingfisher

on a perch above the river

A branch over water is a favorite perch for Belted Kingfishers to look for fish, crayfish, and other prey. The kingfisher may hover in flight before diving into shallow water, then return to its perch with a fish.

Listen for the kingfisher's rattling call as it flies over lakes or rivers. It nests in banks where it can burrow a tunnel more than two feet long. In a chamber at the end of the tunnel, it lays its eggs and cares for its young.

American Kestrel

over farm fields

The American Kestrel is the smallest falcon in North America, about the size of a Mourning Dove. Look for it in open landscapes, such as fields and meadows with trees nearby for nesting and perching. Occasionally a kestrel hovers in the air as it scans for prey such as grasshoppers, beetles, and mice.

Kestrels nest in tree cavities excavated by woodpeckers. They also use nest boxes, enabling them to move into treeless areas such as open prairie.

Sandhill Cranes

dancing

Sandhill Cranes in winter call to one another with deep, throaty cries. Males and females dance, bowing down, then leaping into the air. During courtship, their elaborate performance includes the dance and other coordinated display movements. Sometimes they perform the dance at other times of the year.

Families migrate and spend the winter together. A mated pair stays with their young of the year, sometimes joined by older offspring too. Mates often remain together year after year.

Greater Roadrunner

with Arizona lupine and prickly pear cacti

True to their name, roadrunners have the habit of running along roads—or dry streambeds and other open paths—as fast as 18 miles per hour. Limited in flying ability, they may glide from a perch to the ground or between perches a few yards apart.

The roadrunner's omnivorous diet includes standard fare such as insects, lizards, fruits, and seeds, but it's also undaunted by hairy, spiny, or poisonous prey. It readily eats scorpions, tarantulas, and prickly pear fruit (rolling it first to remove spines), and is known to kill small rattlesnakes.

Barn Owls

with saguaro cacti

Adaptable and widespread, Barn Owls live in a variety of open habitats, including deserts, grasslands, marshes, fields, and towns. They readily nest in natural cavities in trees, cliffs, or caves, as well as in human-made structures such as nest boxes, barns, church steeples, and even Yankee Stadium.

Nocturnal hunters, they are capable of capturing mice in total darkness using only their sense of hearing. This keen hearing also enables them to strike prey under grass or snow.

Black-capped Chickadees
in Douglas-fir

Curious, observant, and sociable, Black-capped Chickadees enliven the woods all year. Long after many songbirds have departed for the winter, chickadees roam in flocks as they search for food and look out for danger.

Their curiosity helps them find the remnants of summer's bounty—silk cases with spider eggs, dormant caterpillars, weed seeds, frozen berries, seeds spilled from cones pried open by nuthatches. They hide extra food in curled leaves, bark, lichens, and clusters of conifer needles and can remember where to retrieve them for as long as a month.

Northern Saw-whet Owl

at her nest cavity

Northern Saw-whet Owls hide so well, they're rarely seen, even though they are one of the most common owls in the forests of southern Canada and the northern United States. No larger than a robin, the saw-whet owl uses its keen hearing to capture mice and other prey at night.

The female lays her eggs in a tree cavity such as a hole excavated by a woodpecker. The male brings food to her while she keeps the eggs warm, sometimes even leaving her with a stash of food (one biologist counted 24 prey items). After the eggs hatch, he brings food for another month until the nestlings get old enough to fly out of the tree cavity.

White-breasted Nuthatch

with maple and paper birch

Defying gravity, a White-breasted Nuthatch climbs down a tree, pausing now and then to probe the bark for insects, larvae, and eggs. Perhaps it will turn up new morsels missed by woodpeckers and other birds that search upward. Unlike a woodpecker, which uses its tail to brace itself against a trunk, the nuthatch clings just with its feet, aided by an oversized back toe.

Nuthatches use the furrows of bark as a larder for hiding food and as holders for shelling seeds. After wedging a seed in place, a nuthatch can freely pound with its bill to remove the shell.

Greater Sage-Grouse
displaying

In the sagebrush country of the American West, a Greater Sage-Grouse performs a spectacular display to attract females. As an audience of female grouse looks on, he struts, fans his tail, and puffs out air sacs in his throat pouch while producing popping and whistling sounds.

Usually one male in the display area wins most of the females. Each female strikes out on her own a week or two later to lay her eggs in a spot concealed by sagebrush or grass. She cares for the eggs and raises her young without any help from the male.

Peregrine Falcon

above the Pacific coast

Peregrine Falcons are masters of flight. When hunting, they may achieve speeds of 200 miles per hour in full stoop. They dive from heights of more than half a mile in the air, free falling with wings tucked in until they suddenly pull up at the bottom of a dive. In this way, they harvest most of their food from the air. They are known to capture more than 429 bird species, ranging in size from hummingbirds to geese.

Some peregrines migrate each year across the continents. Scientists tracked a female peregrine in autumn from Maryland to Guatemala, then Honduras, Nicaragua, Ecuador, Bolivia, and Argentina.

Great Horned Owl

in an oak tree

By day, the mottled plumage of a Great Horned Owl helps it blend into its surroundings. By night, its very soft feathers allow it to fly nearly silently as it hunts for prey. The edges of its wing feathers have comb-like structures that reduce the sounds of air passing over the wing.

Although the two tufts on its head resemble ears, the tufts are only feathers. An owl's ears are lower down on the sides of its head, covered in feathers. The disc-like shape of its face directs sound waves to its ears for the acute hearing it needs to hunt at night.

American Avocet

in open wetland

A graceful American Avocet wades in a wetland, using its long, upcurved bill to catch insects and aquatic plants. Sometimes it jabs quickly with its bill to snatch a morsel spotted near the surface. Other times, it sweeps its bill back and forth in the mud, seeking invertebrates such as amphipods.

Avocets inhabit a variety of wetland habitats throughout the year, including saline lakes in summer and intertidal mudflats in winter. They are active at night as well as during the day—eating, interacting with one another, and mating, whether by the light of the moon or the sun.

Red-winged Blackbird

in "song spread" display

In spring, marshes come to life with the sound of Red-winged Blackbirds contesting territories and wooing mates with their songs, *Onk-a-reee!* The male flashes brilliant red patches on his wings as he sings.

The red patches serve as a signal both to females and to rival males. A male displays his patches during courtship because the color attracts females. He also displays his patches to males to proclaim his status and readiness for combat. He shows off the red when he is singing on his own territory, but when trespassing, he conceals it.

Green-winged Teal

in a cattail marsh

Green-winged Teal travel the continent, migrating from wintering grounds in Mexico and the southern United States to nesting areas in the north, into the boreal forests of Canada. They migrate in flocks, mostly at night.

They come down in wetlands to rest and refuel. Green-winged Teals are one of the smallest ducks in North America and they prefer smaller food than other dabbling ducks. They dip their bills in shallow water to capture insects and seeds of grasses and sedges, aided by finely spaced combs on the inside edge of their bills that serve as strainers.

Tufted Titmice

in a flowering redbud tree

The Tufted Titmouse is a welcome visitor to backyards and feeders throughout the year, endearing because of its expressive crest and large eyes, and entertaining because of its acrobatic maneuvers, hovering among leaves or hanging upside down in search of food.

Ever alert, Tufted Titmice are often the first to scold and mob a predator, drawing attention from other birds nearby to chase it away.

Eastern Bluebird

with dogwood flowers

Bluebirds are even more dazzling to one another than they are to people. Like most other bird species, they can see in the range of near-ultraviolet light. They have brilliant ultraviolet-blue plumage on their heads, backs, wings, and tails. Males reflect more ultraviolet colors than females.

Scientists have found that the most colorful males are more successful. They win better nest sites, bring more food to the nest, and raise more young.

Blackburnian Warbler

in an eastern hemlock

In spring, listen for the high-pitched song of a Blackburnian Warbler for a chance at a prized sighting of this beautiful Neotropical migrant. High in the canopy, it hops along branches, reaching out with its bill to glean insects from leaves, or it hovers to pluck prey from beneath.

After raising a family and leaving the nesting area, Blackburnian Warblers sometimes join flocks of Black-capped Chickadees, Golden-crowned Kinglets, Red-breasted Nuthatches, and other birds as they search the trees for food.

Baltimore Orioles

with red buckeye flowers

Baltimore Orioles enjoy their favorite foods all year long by migrating with the seasons. They feast on fruit and insects, and sip nectar from flowers during spring and summer in the woodlands of the United States and Canada, and winter in the tropics.

The female, an expert weaver, creates a hanging, gourd-shaped nest from grasses, milkweed stems, and grapevine bark. Using her bill, often working upside down, she weaves in one fiber at a time to build a basket with a long neck and an entrance at the top. Sitting inside her handiwork, she lays her eggs and incubates them for 11–14 days. Her mate helps her feed the young when they hatch.

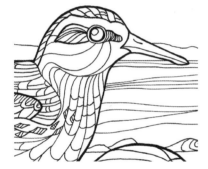

Red Knots

on spring migration

Each year, Red Knots travel more than 9,000 miles from their wintering grounds in Tierra del Fuego at the southern tip of South America to their nesting areas on the arctic tundra.

The Delaware Bay on the Atlantic coast of the United States is a key rest stop and refueling area on their way north in spring. They arrive as horseshoe crabs are coming ashore to spawn. By gorging on the eggs of horseshoe crabs, Red Knots can double their body weight, giving them critical fuel to continue their journeys.

California Quail

and California poppies

California Quail are social birds even before they hatch. Females lay, on average, 8-12 eggs in a nest. Inside the eggs, the embryos make peeping and clicking sounds, and utter a special call just before hatching. These sounds are believed to help the chicks hatch at the same time.

Once hatched, the young are capable of walking around and pecking for food right away. One parent leads them to food while the other perches above, keeping a lookout for hawks and other predators. Two or more families may join and spend the winter together in coveys.

Tree Swallows

at a beaver pond

Acrobatic fliers, Tree Swallows chase after feathers aloft on the wind. They use the feathers to line their nests. The insulation helps keeps the young swallows warm. Studies showed that Tree Swallows fledged earlier from nests with more feathers.

One nest had 105 feathers from at least five duck species, including Northern Pintail, American Wigeon, and Redhead, as well as feathers from Sandhill Cranes.

Painted Bunting

among upright prairie coneflowers

In Spanish, the Painted Bunting is known as "mariposa" (butterfly); in French it is "nonpareil" (without equal). Females and young males are light yellowish green. In their second year, males transform, growing feathers of bright blue, green, and red.

They are birds of open landscapes with scattered trees, shrubs, and grasses, where males sing from tall perches and females build their nests low in shrubs or trees. They eat grasshoppers and caterpillars, along with seeds of bristle grasses, sedges, and wildflowers.

Sources

The primary source of information for this book was *The Birds of North America Online*, published by the Cornell Lab of Ornithology and American Ornithologists' Union at bna.birds.cornell.edu.

Badikova, A. A. and Dzerzhynsky F. Ya. 2015. Functional morphology and adaptive features of the jaw apparatus in puffins (Fraterculini, Alcidae, and Charadriiformes). Biology 42(7): 622–632.

Bent, A. C. 1958. Western Tanager. In Life Histories of North American Blackbirds, Orioles, Tanagers, and Allies. Washington: Smithsonian Institution.

Bonar, R. L. 2000. Availability of Pileated Woodpecker cavities and use by other species. Journal of Wildlife Management 64(1): 52–59.

Bertin, R. I. 1982b. Floral biology, hummingbird pollination, and fruit production of trumpet creeper (*Campsis radicans*, Bignoniaceae). American Journal of Botany 69: 122–134.

Devine A. and Smith, D. G. 2005. Caching behavior by wintering Northern Saw-whet Owls, *Aegolius acadicus*. Canadian Field-Naturalist 119(4): 578–579.

Heinrich, B. 2015. Chickadees in winter. Natural History 123(2): 30–35.

Higuchi, H. 1985. Bait-fishing by the Green-backed Heron *Ardeola striata* in Japan. Ibis 128: 285–290.

Jones, T. M., Rodewald, A. D., and Shustack, D. P. 2010. Variation in plumage coloration in Northern Cardinals in urbanizing landscapes. Wilson Journal of Ornithology 122(2): 236–333.

Munro, J. A., Clinton, G. et al. 1943. Identification of feathers in a Tree Swallow's nest. Condor 45(1): 37–40.

Payne, R. S. Acoustic location of prey by Barn Owls (*Tyto alba*). 1971. Journal of Experimental Biology 54: 535–573.

Siefferman, L. and Hill, G. E. 2005. UV-blue structural coloration and competition for nest boxes in male Eastern Bluebirds. Animal Behaviour 69: 67–72.

Winkler, D. W. 1993. Use and importance of feathers as nest lining in Tree Swallows (*Tachycineta bicolor*). Auk 110(1): 29–36.

Yasukawa, K., Butler, L. K., and Enstrom, D. A. 2009. Intersexual and intrasexual consequences of epaulet colour in male Red-winged Blackbrids: An experimental approach. Animal Behavior 77: 531–540.

Cover: Ruby-throated Hummingbird. Back cover: Great Horned Owl. Page 3: Bald Eagle. Page 5: Blue Jay. Page 6: Rose-breasted Grosbeak. This page: Killdeer.